IN THE BEGINNING

HANS SAMSOM
LAURA ROUS

DERBIBOOKS

DUTCH EDITION © COPYRIGHT 1973 MEULENHOFF INTERNATIONAL
ENGLISH EDITION © COPYRIGHT 1974 MEULENHOFF INTERNATIONAL

1

IN THE BEGINNING GOD CREATED THE HEAVEN AND THE EARTH. 2 AND THE EARTH WAS WITHOUT FORM, AND VOID; AND DARKNESS WAS UPON THE FACE OF THE DEEP. AND THE SPIRIT OF GOD MOVED UPON THE FACE OF THE WATERS. 3 AND GOD SAID, LET THERE BE LIGHT: AND THERE WAS LIGHT. 4 AND GOD SAW THE LIGHT, THAT IT WAS GOOD: AND GOD DIVIDED THE LIGHT FROM THE DARKNESS. 5 AND GOD CALLED THE LIGHT DAY, AND THE DARKNESS HE CALLED NIGHT. AND THE EVENING AND THE MORNING WERE THE FIRST DAY. 6 AND GOD SAID, LET THERE BE A FIRMAMENT IN THE MIDST OF THE WATERS, AND LET IT DIVIDE THE WATERS FROM THE WATERS. 7 AND GOD MADE THE FIRMAMENT, AND DIVIDED THE WATERS WHICH WERE UNDER THE FIRMAMENT FROM THE WATERS WHICH WERE ABOVE THE FIRMAMENT: AND IT WAS SO. 8 AND GOD CALLED THE FIRMAMENT HEAVEN. AND THE EVENING AND THE MORNING WERE THE SECOND DAY. 9 AND GOD SAID, LET THE WATERS UNDER THE HEAVEN BE GATHERED TOGETHER UNTO ONE PLACE, AND LET THE DRY LAND APPEAR: AND IT WAS SO. 10 AND GOD CALLED THE DRY LAND EARTH: AND THE GATHERING TOGETHER OF THE WATERS CALLED HE SEAS: AND GOD SAW THAT IT WAS GOOD. 11 AND GOD SAID, LET THE EARTH BRING FORTH GRASS, THE HERB YIELDING SEED, AND THE FRUIT TREE YIELDING FRUIT AFTER HIS KIND, WHOSE SEED IS IN ITSELF, UPON THE EARTH: AND IT WAS SO. 12 AND THE EARTH BROUGHT FORTH GRASS, AND HERB YIELDING SEED AFTER HIS KIND, AND THE TREE YIELDING FRUIT, WHOSE SEED WAS IN ITSELF, AFTER HIS KIND: AND GOD SAW THAT IT WAS GOOD. 13 AND THE EVENING AND THE MORNING WERE THE THIRD DAY. 14 AND GOD SAID, LET THERE BE LIGHTS IN THE FIRMAMENT OF THE HEAVEN TO DIVIDE THE DAY FROM THE NIGHT; AND LET THEM BE FOR SIGNS, AND FOR SEASONS, AND FOR DAYS, AND YEARS: 15 AND LET THEM BE FOR LIGHTS IN THE FIRMAMENT OF THE HEAVEN TO GIVE LIGHT UPON THE EARTH: AND IT WAS SO. 16 AND GOD MADE TWO GREAT LIGHTS; THE GREATER LIGHT TO RULE THE DAY, AND THE LESSER LIGHT TO RULE THE NIGHT: HE MADE THE STARS ALSO. 17 AND GOD SET THEM IN THE FIRMAMENT OF THE HEAVEN TO GIVE LIGHT UPON THE EARTH, 18 AND TO RULE OVER THE DAY AND OVER THE NIGHT, AND TO DIVIDE THE LIGHT FROM THE DARKNESS: AND GOD SAW THAT IT WAS GOOD. 19 AND THE EVENING AND THE MORNING WERE THE FOURTH DAY. 20 AND GOD SAID, LET THE WATERS BRING FORTH ABUNDANTLY THE MOVING CREATURE THAT HATH LIFE, AND FOWL THAT MAY FLY ABOVE THE EARTH IN THE OPEN FIRMAMENT OF HEAVEN. 21 AND GOD CREATED GREAT WHALES, AND EVERY LIVING CREATURE THAT MOVETH, WHICH THE WATERS BROUGHT FORTH ABUNDANTLY, AFTER THEIR KIND, AND EVERY WINGED FOWL AFTER HIS KIND: AND GOD SAW THAT IT WAS GOOD. 22 AND GOD BLESSED THEM, SAYING, BE FRUITFUL, AND MULTIPLY, AND FILL THE WATERS IN THE SEAS, AND LET FOWL MUL-

TIPLY IN THE EARTH. 23 AND THE EVENING AND THE MORNING WERE THE FIFTH DAY. 24 AND GOD SAID, LET THE EARTH BRING FORTH THE LIVING CREATURE AFTER HIS KIND, CATTLE, AND CREEPING THING, AND BEAST OF THE EARTH AFTER HIS KIND: AND IT WAS SO. 25 AND GOD MADE THE BEAST OF THE EARTH AFTER HIS KIND, AND CATTLE AFTER THEIR KIND, AND EVERYTHING THAT CREEPETH UPON THE EARTH AFTER HIS KIND: AND GOD SAW THAT IT WAS GOOD. 26 AND GOD SAID, LET US MAKE MAN IN OUR IMAGE, AFTER OUR LIKENESS: AND LET THEM HAVE DOMINION OVER THE FISH OF THE SEA, AND OVER THE FOWL OF THE AIR, AND OVER THE CATTLE, AND OVER ALL THE EARTH, AND OVER EVERY CREEPING THING THAT CREEPETH UPON THE EARTH. 27 SO GOD CREATED MAN IN HIS OWN IMAGE, IN THE IMAGE OF GOD CREATED HE HIM; MALE AND FEMALE CREATED HE THEM. 28 AND GOD BLESSED THEM, AND GOD SAID UNTO THEM, BE FRUITFUL, AND MULTIPLY, AND REPLENISH THE EARTH, AND SUBDUE IT: AND HAVE DOMINION OVER THE FISH OF THE SEA, AND OVER THE FOWL OF THE AIR, AND OVER EVERY LIVING THING THAT MOVETH UPON THE EARTH. 29 AND GOD SAID, BEHOLD, I HAVE GIVEN YOU EVERY HERB BEARING SEED, WHICH IS UPON THE FACE OF ALL THE EARTH, AND EVERY TREE, IN THE WHICH IS THE FRUIT OF A TREE YIELDING SEED; TO YOU IT SHALL BE FOR MEAT. 30 AND TO EVERY BEAST OF THE EARTH, AND TO EVERY FOWL OF THE AIR, AND TO EVERY THING THAT CREEPETH UPON THE EARTH, WHEREIN THERE IS LIFE, I HAVE GIVEN EVERY GREEN HERB FOR MEAT: AND IT WAS SO. 31 AND GOD SAW EVERY THING THAT HE HAD MADE, AND, BEHOLD, IT WAS VERY GOOD. AND THE EVENING AND THE MORNING WERE THE SIXTH DAY.

2 THUS THE HEAVENS AND THE EARTH WERE FINISHED, AND ALL THE HOST OF THEM. 2 AND ON THE SEVENTH DAY GOD ENDED HIS WORK WHICH HE HAD MADE; AND HE RESTED ON THE SEVENTH DAY FROM ALL HIS WORK WHICH HE HAD MADE. 3 AND GOD BLESSED THE SEVENTH DAY, AND SANCTIFIED IT: BECAUSE THAT IN IT HE HAD RESTED FROM ALL HIS WORK WHICH GOD CREATED AND MADE. 4 THESE ARE THE GENERATIONS OF THE HEAVENS AND OF THE EARTH WHEN THEY WERE CREATED, IN THE DAY THAT THE LORD GOD MADE THE EARTH AND THE HEAVENS, 5 AND EVERY PLANT OF THE FIELD BEFORE IT WAS IN THE EARTH, AND EVERY HERB OF THE FIELD BEFORE IT GREW: FOR THE LORD GOD HAS NOT CAUSED IT TO RAIN UPON THE EARTH, AND THERE WAS NOT A MAN TO TILL THE GROUND. 6 BUT THERE WENT UP A MIST FROM THE EARTH, AND WATERED THE WHOLE FACE OF THE GROUND. 7 AND THE LORD GOD FORMED MAN OF THE DUST OF THE GROUND, AND BREATHED INTO HIS NOSTRILS THE BREATH OF LIFE; AND MAN BECAME A LIVING SOUL.

DEEP.

AND GOD SAID, LET THERE BE LIGHT: AND THERE WAS LIGHT.

AND THE EVENING AND THE MORNING WERE THE FIRST DAY.

...LET THERE BE A FIRMAMENT IN THE MIDST OF THE WATERS, AND LET IT DIVID
SECOND DAY.

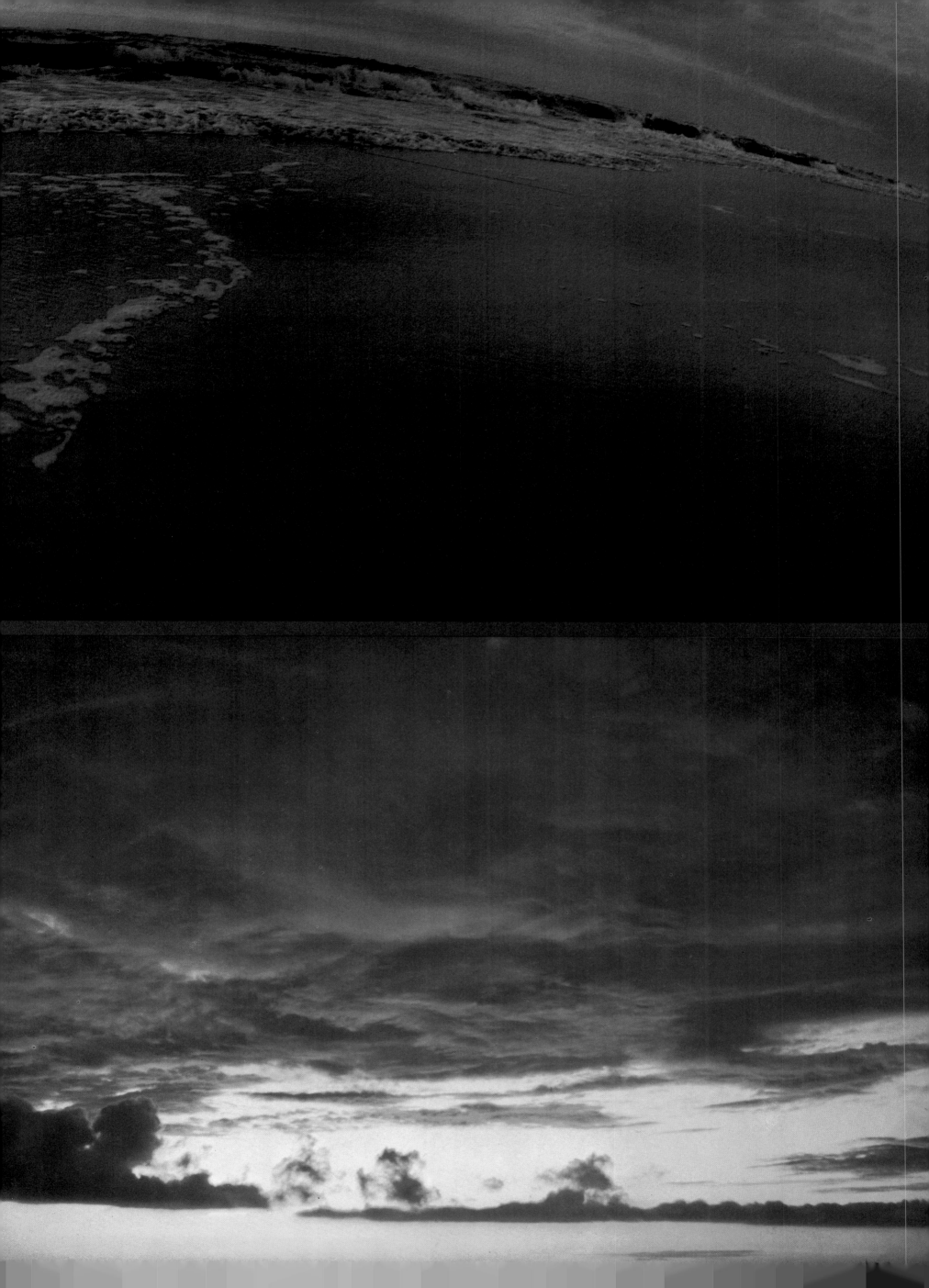

ND LET THE DRY LAND APPEAR: AND IT WAS SO.

AND GOD SAID, LET THERE BE LIGHTS IN THE FIRMAMENT OF THE HEAVEN TO DIVID
AND FOR DAYS, AND YEARS.

HE DAY FROM THE NIGHT; AND LET THEM BE FOR SIGNS, AND FOR SEASONS

AND THE EVENING AND THE MORNING WERE THE FOURTH DAY.

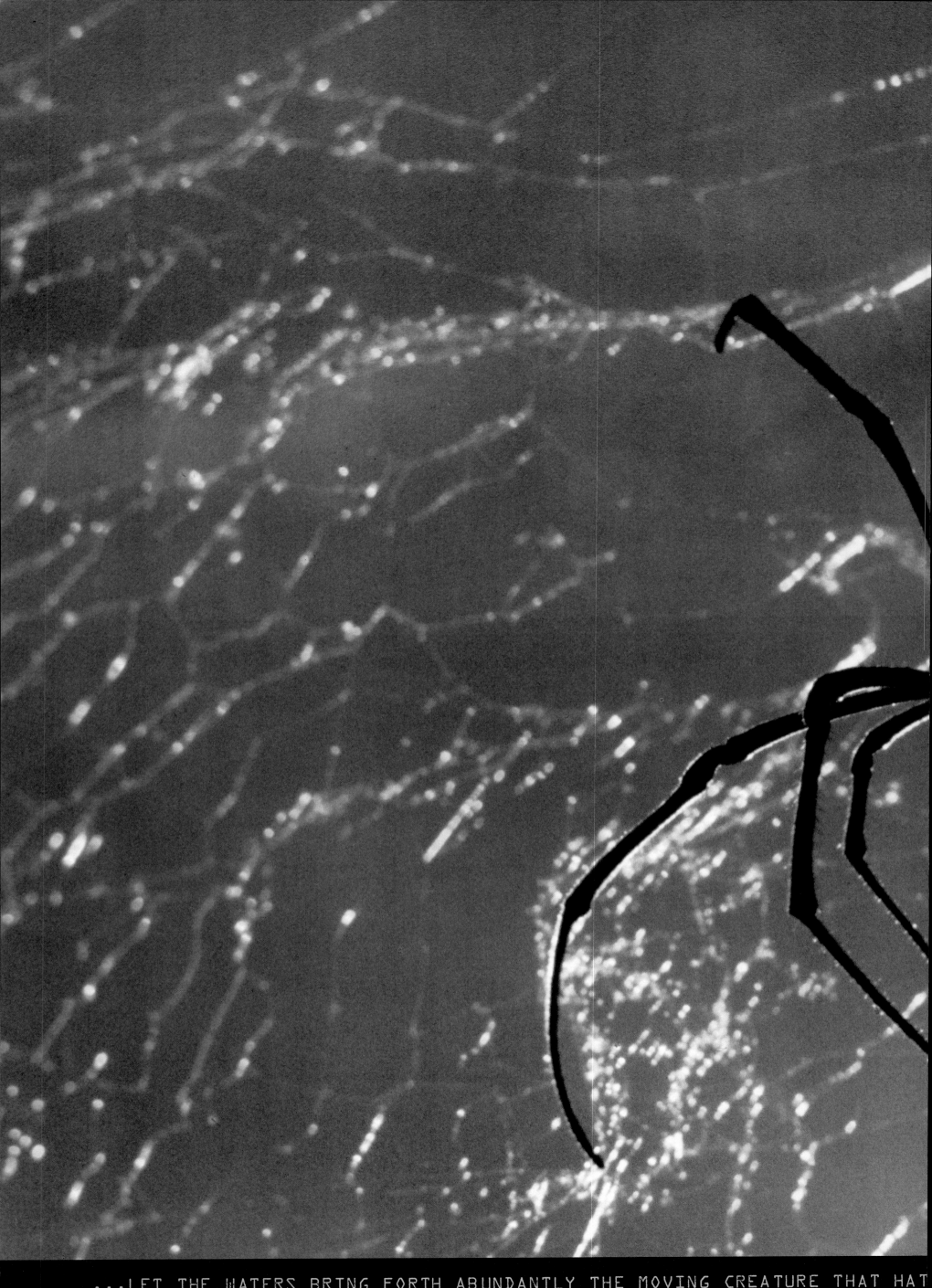

...LET THE WATERS BRING FORTH ABUNDANTLY THE MOVING CREATURE THAT HAT
THE HEAVEN.   AND THE EVENING AND THE MORNING WERE THE FIFTH DAY.

LET THE EARTH BRING FORTH THE LIVING CREATURE AFTER HIS KIND, CATTLE, AN

SREATED MAN IN HIS OWN IMAGE ... IN THE IMAGE OF GOD CREATED HE HI

...AND FEMALE CREATED HE THEM.

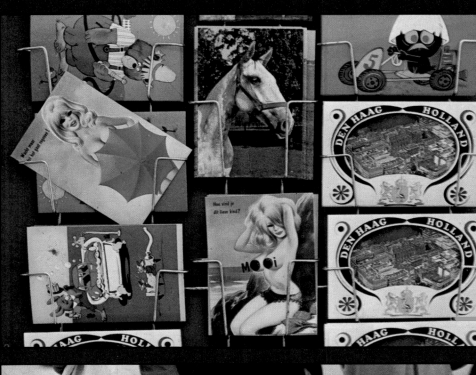

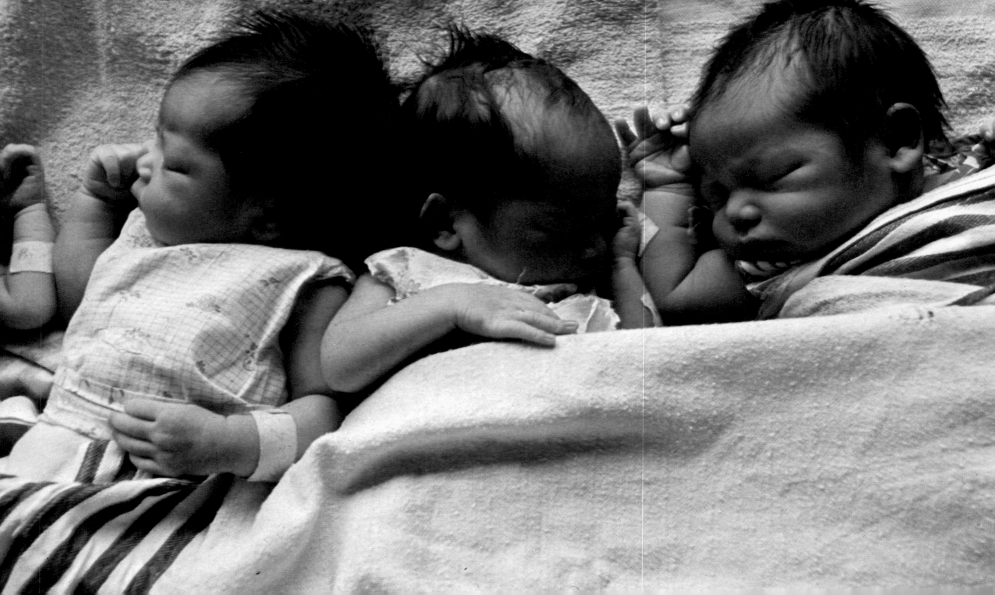

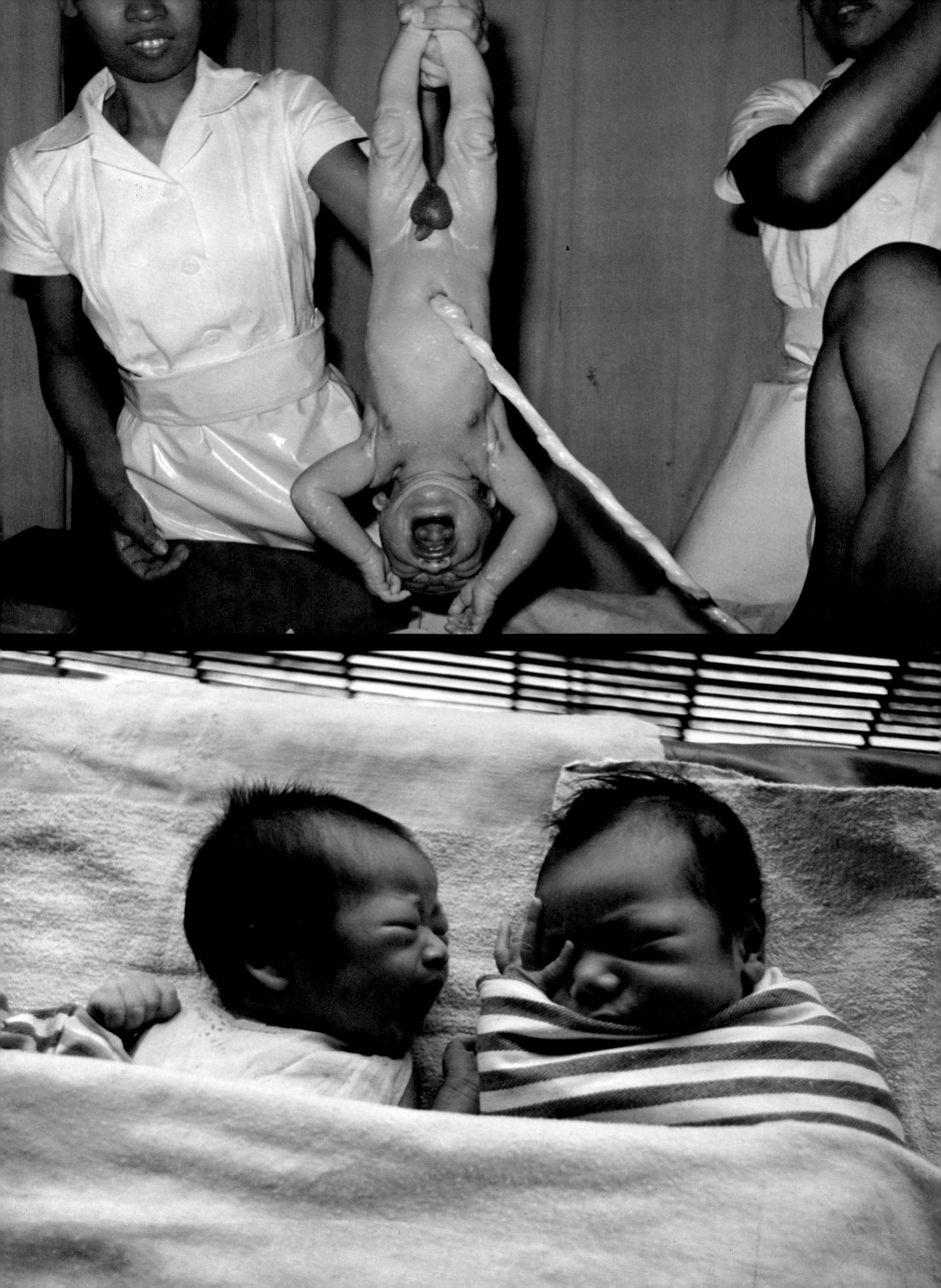

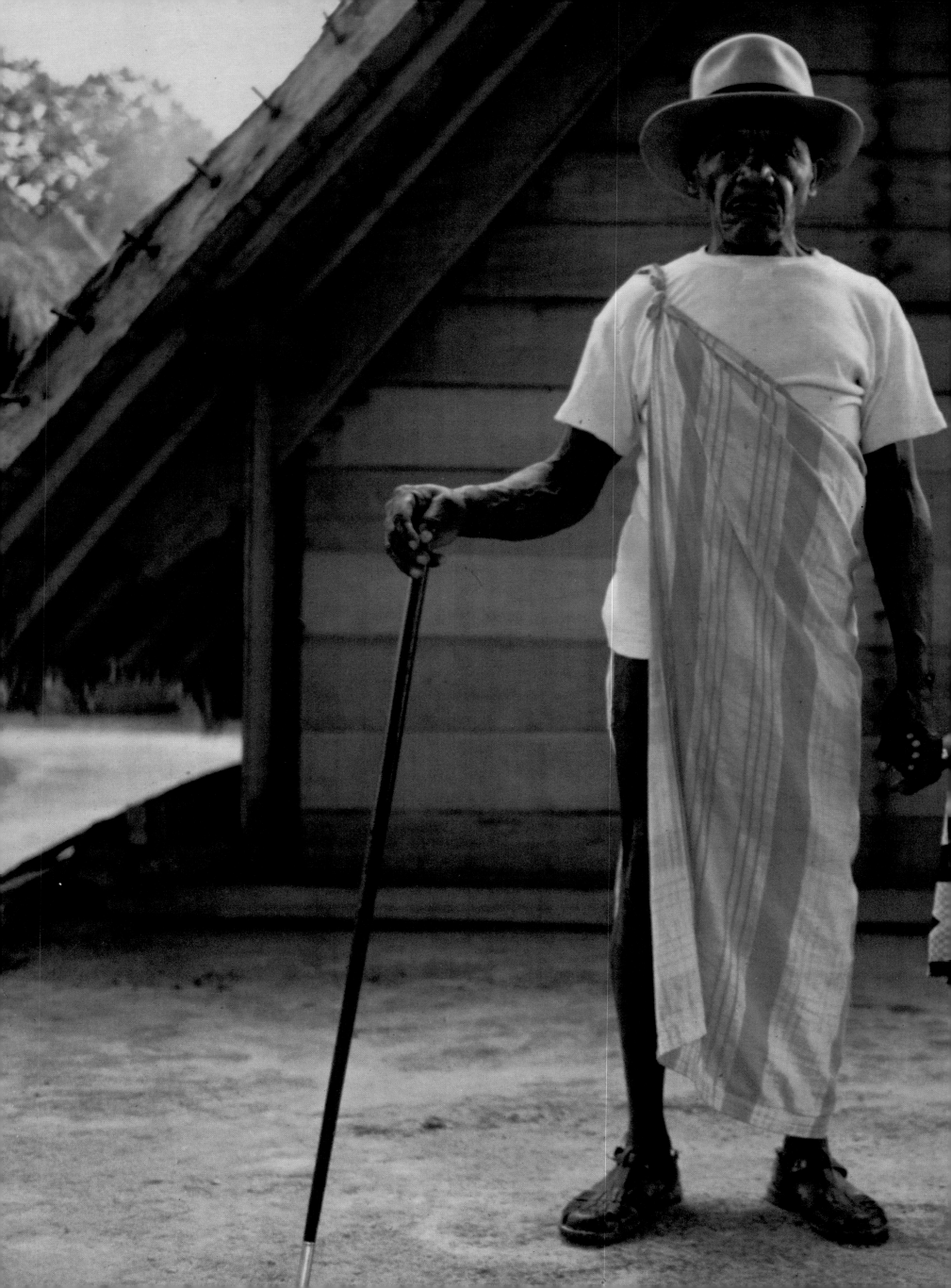

BE FRUITFUL, AND MULTIPLY...

AND REPLENISH THE EARTH, AND SUBDUE IT.

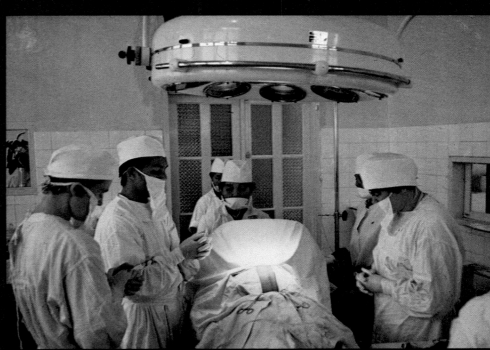

AND REPLENISH THE EARTH, AND SUBDUE IT.

...BEHOLD, I HAVE GIVEN YOU EVERY HERB BEARING SEED, WHICH IS UPON THE FACE
YIELDING SEED; TO YOU IT SHALL BE FOR MEAT.

F ALL THE EARTH, AND EVERY TREE, IN WHICH IS THE FRUIT OF A TREE

...TO YOU IT SHALL BE FOR MEAT.

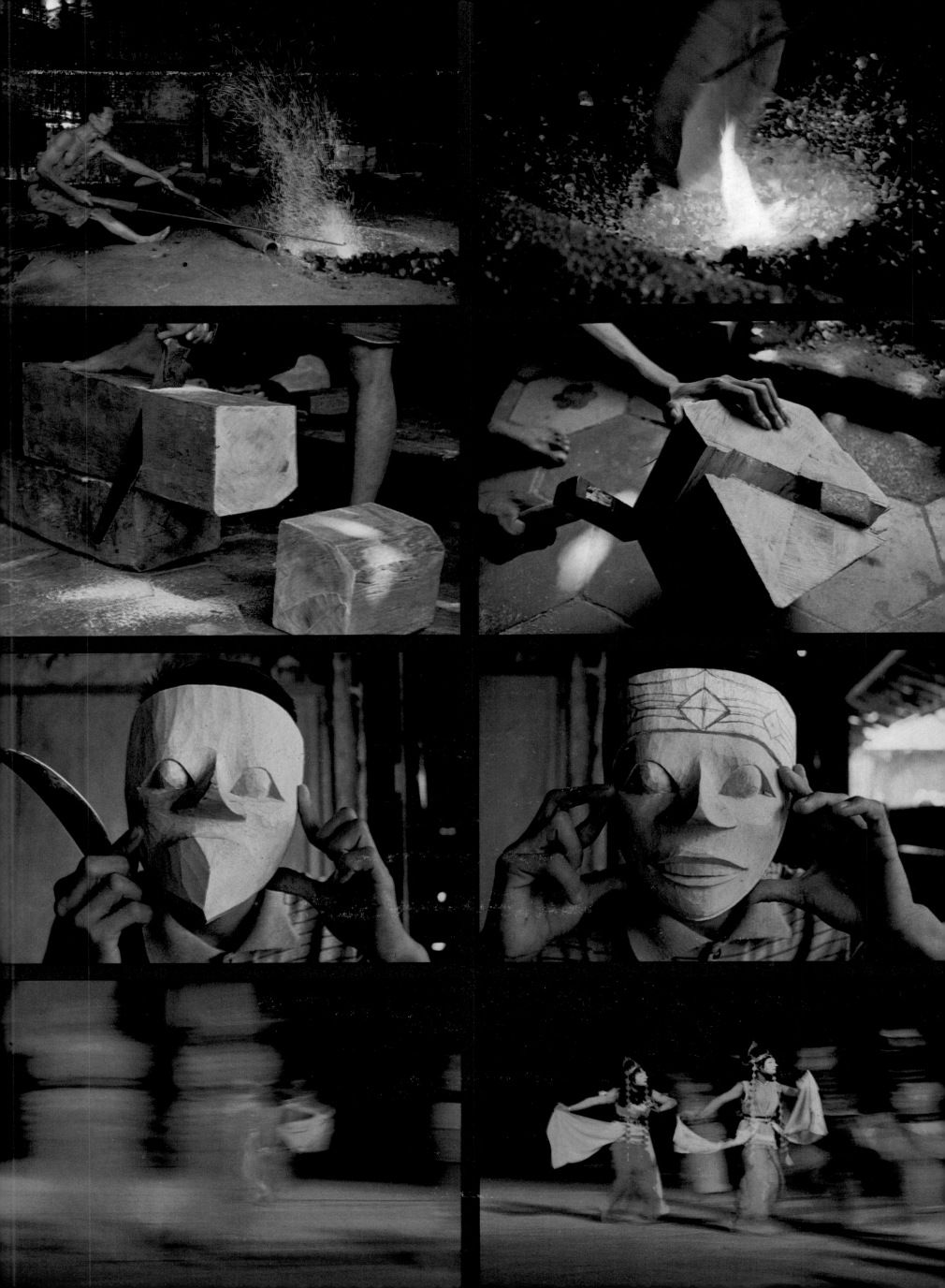

AND GOD BLESSED THE SEVENTH DAY, AND SANCTIFIED IT...

A LOURDES
NOUS AVONS PRIÉ POUR TOI

AND SANCTIFIED IT...

AND SANCTIFIED IT...

AND SANCTIFIED IT...

...AND MAN BECAME A LIVING SOUL.

PUBLISHED BY:

DERBIBOOKS, INC. 110 ENTERPRISE AVENUE, SECAUCUS, NEW JERSEY 07094

BY ARRANGEMENT WITH HUGH LAUTER LEVIN ASSOCIATES

I.S.B.N. 0-89009-013-0